Please Hold

Please Hold

Poems

Dave Cavanagh

Fomite
Burlington VT

ISBN-13: 978-1-967022-10-6
Library of Congress Control Number: 2025946770

Fomite
58 Peru Street
Burlington, VT 05401

02-16-2026

For my family and friends
and for all those who read books

Poetry by Dave Cavanagh

More about Dave's writing at dave.cavanagh.com

Contents

Foyer

Does a book of poems need a preface? Perhaps not. But perhaps it can help, the way a front walkway, porch, or foyer of a house can ease the way into the interior, make one feel welcome.

You can think of this book as a kind of dwelling. I open it to you even as you literally have opened it and, I hope, will open *to* it. Each poem is a room or furnishing with a particular texture, color, shape, sound, purpose. Is there a unifying framework for this building? To my mind there very much is, but I leave that for you to experience. In any case, I hope you feel engaged, connected, with some or many of the poems.

So welcome to *Please Hold*. And thank you. Each poem may offer the possibility of connection, but it needs you to reach inside and make it happen.

Coming or Going

C'mon, c'mon, c'mon,
   honk the flyover geese,
         necks stretched out
with purpose. They fly their loose
   communal V.

      A single, raucous caw
from a high-perched unseen crow.
      An answer from a far field.
Then silence. Assurance of some sort,
      enough to carry on.

   Their lives are crisp,
unwasted. They seem to know
      what to do, and when. Time takes
their lead, dissolves. Consider this
      my caw.

Love-Tossed

Passing

So many I know passing away.
The euphemism I sniffed at for so long
revealed now as precise. I'm walking

still by water. A mottled leaf floats past
on the silent current. A chickadee lands,
leaps from a branch. Moss greens itself

on shaded rock. Sojourners on the move,
crisscrossing, layering, reaching. And you,
such good company, together in passing.

"Be Your Own Boss"

A terrible idea, seductive but silly,
at least for me, a decent man but prone
to dither and overthink, until trouble
sprouts and possibility leaves town.

Long blessed by strong women bosses,
I pine now for the muses. Don't leave
me unattended. I can't be trusted
here alone. My own devices pale.

Without you my days yawn; my leaves wilt,
my streams run dry; my streets grow hot
with clamor. Boss me, ladies, please.
Clap and I'll hear water, air, their song.

I know you're here somewhere. I'm all
eyes for your beck, all ears for your call.

Choice Hotel

Swing from dream's rafters, careen
      through hallways that tilt
   and never quite connect.

Loved ones fill the bar. Many of them
      dead but cheerful,
  beckoning. A chair

   for me at every table. Where to sit?
A forever question. Choose one,
     leave the others out.

Sit alone at the bar instead.
    "What'll it be?" says the bartender,
       "we serve cocktails and fairytales."

One of each, maybe. One of each, I guess.

Paint Job

I've said all I should, painted the porch
till the can is empty, only syrupy
dregs of gray left at the bottom.

But the porch, fit for a visitor. An ancestor,
maybe, or my dead brother, someone
who can explain but most likely will not.

Someone who will smile, reach out a hand
as if to say, okay, you used your head
like you were told. Now paint the rest –

all those peeling walls and doors,
especially the doors – with all the colors
you don't know you have, or avoid

because no name. All those terrifying
darks and lights. They're all you've got now.
Gray is gone. Finally no choice but to choose.

About the Size of It

I've shrunk an inch.
The spongebobs between bones
drying out, no doubt,
shriveling into soup crackers.
Or the backbone bowing,
the whole stalwart frame
nodding to time and gravity.
Maybe growing weary, too,
bearing up my worlds so long --
the one given, the one encountered,
especially the one imagined.

Though these days thoughts
fly off almost as fast as they hatch.
I keep having to chase and haul
them back. When I was young
they weighed me down.
So serious, knotted, laden.
It must be their fault I am short.
But I forgive them, they didn't
know they had a choice, and so
they didn't. Now I've come to see

the lightness of all things, how
gravity depends in part on where
you stand on earth, and laughter
the best leavening of all. Every
day I try to practice a light touch.
By night I am a star hoops player
in dreams, as in my timid teenage

years quickness and court sense
made the game an unlikely refuge,
a safe space on an open stage.
Lost in motion, or found,
I weaved at ease among the tall.

In night games now, I stretch out
horizontal. I spread the weight,
slow down the play. By morning
I've grown back half an inch.
I have to laugh, rise up,
begin to shrink again.

A Canadian/American Hears a Recording of T.S. Eliot

Seldom can I hear the native "oot"
in my "about." My Yankee friends think
it's a hoot. So I wonder how Old Possum
torqued his St. Louis tongue into starched
faux-Brit locutions. Was it natural erosion?
I have my doots. You might even say
I'm from Missouri. I love Mr. Prufrock's
song, but hearing Mr. E's rendition,
I long for him to own where he began
and marry it to where he chose to be.
No good to say the emotion of art
is impersonal, that poems are escape
from personality. There's no flight out
from that geography. It lives in you,
you in it. I too grow old. All my Canuck/
Doodle Dandy sounds, all my molecules
recombine. New bell-song with old beats.
And one thing more: If I can hear
the mermaids singing, even if only
each to each and not to me, I'll marvel
at their sea-borne intonations.
What more could I want, or need?

Housefly

Back, forth, up, across, madly buzzing
inside the window screen; with two antennae,
six legs and thousands of eyes unable to find
the opening I've made for it down below.

I get it, having done plenty of pointless back-
and-forth myself. If freedom could talk, it'd yell,
"Are you kidding? What more do you need?
Look around, man, go. Go!"

Unless

Fly is a scientist, meticulous, with antennae
that can smell and compound eyes examining
this strange structure that lets in air but does not
let him out, its delicately gridded surface

like the tiniest prison bars. Or she's a philosopher
of the fly world, reflecting how life's breezes
mingle with one's choices and lead to puzzling
enclosures that may in time turn deadly.

Until

Fly turns activist in desperation and looks
where it has not looked before, sees what eyes
too used to cross-hatched view could not,
remembers that other wonder of its nature – wings!

Fly's gone. Thanks be. With only a few weeks

on earth, hours trapped inside seemed a waste.
Unless it learned something, maybe to pass on.
I close down the screen before its sibling comes.

Flying from Montgomery

For my brother Pat, RIP 2016
and John Prine, RIP 2020

Last days of cancer and you played
    John's song for us.
Your voice soft and low, frail fingers
    fretting the old chords,
light glinting off the sunburst guitar.
    "Just give me one thing
that I can hold on to…" A song of depression,
    you said, and sad-sweet sang it
into something more, as all art does,
    as life well lived
can do. *"To believe in this livin'*
    is just a hard way to go."
Soon leaving, you left us belief
    in the struggle to believe.
Your smile as you sang so gentle, shy
    but sure, an early morning lake.
Now John's gone, too. The Sea of Covid
    took him. You never met but
somehow knew each other well. Good night,
    sweet princes, flights of angels
sing thee as you've sung, and in asking
    shown us how to fly.

To the Person Who Broke into My Car Last Night

Strange, I think, the driver's seat pushed way back.
And empty the little bin where I stockpile quarters
for parking. Then it dawns. I must have left
the doors unlocked. You must have sat here
where I'm sitting. You must be tall.
Thank you for not trashing the glove box
you shuffled through. Or anything, really.
Just a few things moved about here or there.
How long did you sit here, checking nooks
and crannies for cash or whatever's sellable,
just as I am now for what's missing?
Not long, I suppose, but who knows,
maybe you stretched back and relaxed,
leaned into the headrest, or stared through
the windshield to the lamplit street,
savored the dark quiet of your moment,
took some time to think. About what, I wonder?
No surprise you made off with the umbrella.
It was a wet night, wet and cold.

Blue Plastic Radio

He is slumped, a melted bottle shape.
Clutches a blue plastic radio, sinks
day by day into the sidewalk he lives on.

He holds it like an orphan's hand,
holds it like a man who needs
to hold an orphan's hand.

Holds it like it's a savior come too late.
Holds it like a shriek, like a memory,
like a mickey. Holds it like he has forgotten

he is holding it, and he holds it
like a rusted stiff old vice.
No tinny tune from it, no wild rhythm.

No sound at all from the radio
he holds onto like everything
he may have once imagined.

Except an outstretched cup.
He does not hold it like a cup
and he does not look up for pity

or any easy coin. Hunches over it,
head tucked away from the crowd
that tries and tries not to look at him.

Fist and a silent blue radio held
like a talisman, a shield, a signature,
an unopened letter.

The Recycle Man

Every groove in the sidewalk announces his passing. The clatter of a shopping cart bulging with black trash bags of returnables hanging over the sides — beer, soda (5 cents each), the occasional whisky or gin bottle (15 cents!). At least twice a day he rattles by in red gym pants and ball cap, arms out straight in front of him, leaning into the push, the pace barely slowed by his loud, sticky load.

He covers miles around town, but our street is home ground. Home? He hails from Vietnam, has little English, as I learn one day when I put out my leavings just as he passes. "Vietnam — no money," he explains, repeats. After weeks of unseen exchanges, we're happy to meet face to face. We labor over words but gladly connect with eyes, broken phrases. He lives down the block with his sister and ailing mother. Who knows what troubles they've fled, the struggles they grapple with now? He is undaunted. Day after day he clacks by, stoops for the leftovers of privilege. Against mean odds, his care, his cheer, his forward lean as he carts our empties to the redemption center.

I give him beer cans; he gives me his creased smile with all that lives within it. His hands come together with a slight bow of thanks. I smile and bow awkwardly back. I hope he knows I owe him.

Elderchild

After decades in life's womb,
    slow passage through
the birth canal of days, here I am,
    my own child, bawling,
crawling, pointing, my babble
    now trying the twisty
turns of talk. A shock how
    arduous at times
the journey, learning to manage
    the furls and thrusts
of my own tongue, shuck off
    the hand-me-down
jabber of the crowd. Or how
    the truest self resists
its own becoming, yet loves
    the shifting tones
and timbres of the resounding world.
    How in an unsought
moment, or with trial and longing,
    a vibration,
a whorl of something wondrous,
    new speech,
forms in the throat, lets loose.

Love-Tossed

I left God at the altar when it dawned
They were infinitely careless
and never would love the likes of me.

God left me altered but still wanting.
I've been looking everywhere. Primroses
by a cracked sidewalk — yellow, insistent,
jubilant, rooted, reaching. A pantheon!

Much more like it. I'm searching the same
earth I'm made of. Everything an aisle,
everything busy being itself, everything a vow.

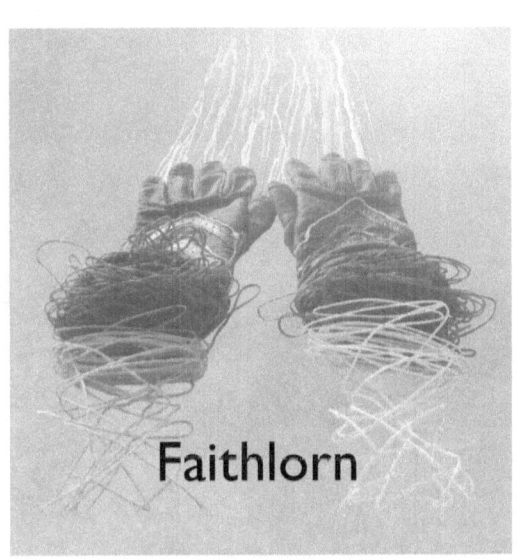

Faithlorn

Ash Wednesday

This year for Lent
I'm giving up
giving up.

Losses worn long
threadbare us all.
Bone chill, the pallor

of ash, what's left
that will not burn.
I'm trying to turn

toward all else
that in time's fire
makes heat and light.

Answer to a Prayer

Your call is important to Us. It's just
    Us Three here
on line 1 (press 1 if you're Christian).
    Actually, everyone
gets told to press 1 — Jews, Moslems,
    Hindus, Buddhists, pagans,
even atheists (go figure) – all think
    they're on line 1.
Anyway, three in one, that's Us,
    a three-fer, like a tri-light
or a tricycle. An odd family, dad, son,
    and whatever. No women,
which is a sadness. They all left.
    Not sure why,
something about tired of waiting,
    something about
a seat at the table. What table?

But your call. Important to Us.
    Except we never really
get the call, you know. Just inklings.
    Too many middlemen,
in-betweeners, all those vestments,
    bell ringings and what-nots,
especially what's in your own head.
    A lot of, what do you call it,
interference, static, noise. Anyway,
    all our associates are busy.
The order in which it was received,
    and so on. Problem is,

big backlog. If it was up to Us.
     Important. Stay on the line.
Estimated wait time, well, never mind.

What matters, you called. It makes Us
     happy, or at least
less lonely, less bored. Really *you're*
     the answer to a prayer.
Don't hang up. Whatever you do,
     stay on the line.
For God's sake, please hold.

"Knock, and it shall be opened..."
−Matthew 7:7

I rapped hard on God's front door. I was such a child.
I thought I'd be let in. I knocked and knocked.
My little fist against carved oak. Finally
a priest – his black robe, the collar notched
to show a starched white square pointing up
to his Adam's apple — cracked the high,
thick portal just enough to step outside
and slap me hard across the face.

Who did I think I was, pounding the Lord's door
like that? I stared and could not say I only wanted
to see inside. Cheeks aflame – one from pain,
both from shame – and an unfamiliar heat, too,
in a down deep place. Even at eight I burned.
Who was this God whose man would beat a child?
I turned away and though I later entered
many times, I never did return.

Faithlorn

I back-burnered faith,
    I corner-of-the-eyed it,
I shy-at-the-partied it

till it got tired of waiting,
    strolled off with the earnests,
the new agers, the hallelordies.

Now I'm all yearning,
    a lonely aloofer
in love beyond belief.

It's a Slog

...coming back to faith.
Easy to believe in Nothing.
Even easier to take up with God.
Like two boxers in their corners,
God in golden, blinding regalia,
Nothing in dark matter, both
puffing their chests, jabbing
the air, hamming it for the crowd,
for me, my quavery soul. They're
keen to have me stamp and shout.
Or not. Big egos don't care much.

I dunno. Dark matter is still matter.
God's duds shine for many. I squint
to see within. The universal gymnasium
plays host. Big ring. Getting bigger.
How much depends on the spyglass
we cobble together. Hubble, hubble,
toil and trouble, when shall we all
meet again? When the worms
have had their way. By then,
who or what is there to know?
 It's a slog coming back to faith.

Bravery

Bending to pull on boots
day after day in life's winter.

Stooping to help a small child
into a parka, mittens pinned

to sleeves like small pectoral
fins, or fledgling wings.

Lost, Found

Just like your house keys, but heavier,
faith has gone missing. You feel for it
in all your inner pockets. Nothing.
You check your mind's shelves stuffed
with favorite beliefs, the end tables
littered with opinions, all the likely places.
You ransack drawers, upstairs dressers
full of folded convictions, memory's back
porch crammed with weathered certitudes.
You try to remember when you saw it last.
You scroll through your routines. But unlike
keys that at last reappear by the same magic
they used to vanish, faith may not turn up.

More like a coin, then, seeming lost for good.
Maybe one day, when you've given up,
or when deep trouble of some kind
strips away all else, there it is, buried in a sofa,
or tucked inside a simple wooden box with old
photos, the one of your parents with three boys.
There all along. You turn it over in your hands,
a strange familiar currency and a small swell
of energy. How did you get along without it?
You promise from now on you'll take care.
You'll keep faith in a safe place, a breast pocket
of the soul, close to your heart. You'll check for it
every day. You'll never lose it again. You promise.

Ark of the Lost Covenant

Those old stone tablets with the Big Ten list,
Thou Shalt Nots and Thou Shalts (mostly Nots),
that Moses hauled down from on high
to keep us all in line. Where did they go?
Wandered off with faith, perhaps, or hope.
Some say a church in Ethiopia, Our Lady Mary
of Zion. Others claim the Temple Mount
in old Jerusalem. That's far.

Where does faith go when it goes?
It leaves behind a broken home, shattered
windows, flapping shutters, doors blown open.
No wonder so many fall back on a stony code
of don'ts and do's against the inner storm.

I go down the list. So far it seems I'm skirting
the eternal burn pit, but nowhere do I see
a gentler bidding, harder than old stone:
"Be kind," "Forgive," "Give yourself a break."
A desert yet to cross. I have a big TV for streaming.
Another documentary on sacred whereabouts.
The wounded, working heart — the most
holy site I know. Its beats, its battered truths
I try to attend, decipher, hold.

Force

for Janet and Patrick

A young friend died last night.
Our planet streaks through space
at a godless pace. Walking its crust,
I can't tell; I guess it's so, but who knows
why it whirls? A young friend died last night,
a fact mysterious as any galactic spin.
The gravity of the sun, sure, and the simple
boggling truth that nothing in space,
not even air, has got in the way to stop
Earth's billions-year-old dash. There must
be more to the story. Some force beyond

the few we know so far of nature. Some
force beyond force, beyond beyond,
and way beyond the mind's small
ruminations. I squint in the brazen
light of spring. Janet died last night,
her whirling done. Or lost to us.
Inexplicable as grief. Where it lives
before we feel it, where it goes.
Or you, this morning, your sadness
stretching a hand across a bedsheet
to mine, the unseen air between us,
the air that we still breathe,
and where our lives still meet.

Windows

Writing a book of poems is an act of faith, or a plea for faith. So is reading a book of poems, or it can be. Before it's a book, and before many of the poems within it exist, a whole lot of staring out of windows goes on. How long can one stare out the window? A long time, it turns out. It may seem that not much is going on. That may be the case. It may also be that a great deal is going on, that staring out the window allows the mind to relax so that deeper processes can get to work.

Work? It's also very sophisticated play. Deep mind wanders, drifts, then bolts, makes lightning collages, stoops for the tiniest details, sweeps the horizon, collapses and expands time. It gathers what the conscious mind cannot grasp, or not yet. Until enough pressure builds, or disparate glimmers coalesce. What was under the surface moves up top, comes into view, and something more than staring happens. Maybe a poem begins to happen. Maybe a book happens.

I've used the word "may" or "maybe" here several times. Really I don't know how a poem happens. Does anyone? Elsewhere I have written about how creativity happens out of the corner of the eye. Look too directly, at least early in the process, and the creative possibility disappears, dissolves, flees. Keep it in view but without staring, with a curious blend of trying/not trying, and you may be able to sidle up to it, or it may sidle up to you.

I may foolishly be saying directly what should only be suggested or implied, left open-ended. There is more than one kind of open-endedness. For example, you can simply open the window and let in what may, even if it is strange, only partly understood, though somehow compelling. There is also the kind that reaches out a hand, or a poem, without knowing whether it will be grasped by another.

What in the World

Nuclear Football

*...the nickname for the 45-pound briefcase that accompanies the
U.S. President at all times when away from a command center. Its
contents can be used to authorize a nuclear attack.*

Only the President can put the ball in play.
Carries a laminated ID card with codes
to verify that he (or someday she) is
quarterback supreme. The card is known
as "the biscuit." Once Clinton misplaced
the biscuit for months. When Reagan was shot
and rushed into surgery, the biscuit turned up
later in his shoe on the floor of the ER.
Most of the time the football gets carried
by an officer with top security clearance
called "Yankee White." At the White House,
the President has the Oval Office,
the Resolute Desk, the Situation Room.
The nuclear football is tucked away. Is it
coincidence that a football is oval?
That football is the U.S.'s most popular sport?
That the teams line up against each other
like armies crouched for an attack? If
the President is resolute, if he makes the call,
who will be able to call timeout? Who will
know until there's no more point in knowing
of the Hail Mary launch into the end zone?

Money Talks

I live with you. You think about me all the time. I seldom think of you.

You made me. You wanted me and you made me.

I started out a useful tool. Helped you trade goods, pleasantries, trust. I brought home the bacon.

Your rich imagination — that's where I came from. But now you only imagine getting rich.

You've dirtied me. You've lied and raped and killed for me.

You've laundered me. A lot of me hides in offshore accounts. Just like your days, they're numbered.

I once was bullion. Then coin. Then paper. Then plastic. Then pixel. I'm more and more cryptic.

I used to sit snug in your wallet. Now I never know where I am, what I am.

I get more and more remote. Or is that you?

An object of desire. A power play. A starch for ego. That's what I am to you.

What will you not do for me? Almost nothing. But not for me. For you. Always just for you.

Sometimes I think I'm going out of fashion. I've lost currency. But no, there you are again, grasping. You want to have your way with me.

You keep careful ledgers of my movements. You count and count me. I can't count on you.

You're drunk on me. I'm wasted.

I keep you awake at night. But you're no fun anymore. If it's not worry, it's scheming. If not scheming, fawning. I hate fawning.

No matter how much of me you possess, you feel poor. You can never get enough of me.

You move as if you're in control, but in the backroom of your psyche you shiver. Your days are a tight tourniquet. You shoot up dollar lust.

You think you're buying time with me, but really you're selling it. Either way, you're running low.

Fear too often buys the gun. Fear fingers the trigger. Fear shrieks
with the flash. Fear at the register. Fear in the hall. Fear in the class.
Fear in the bedroom. Fear on the stoop. Fear in the parking lot.
Fear in the park. Fear in the chapel.
Fear at the club. Fear
with a badge. Fear
on the run. Fear
breeds, bleeds at
both ends of a gun.

*Four in ten adults in the U.S. live in a household with a gun. A major-
ity of them say it's to protect themselves and their families. Yet having
a gun in the house nearly triples the risk that someone there will die
by homicide. Regarding suicide, the risk is eight times higher for men
and 35 times higher for women compared with non-gun-owners. – Pew
Research Center, 2019; New England Journal of Medicine, 1993, 2020.*

November 25, 2023, 6:25 pm, Burlington, Vermont

*Three young Palestinian men visiting over Thanksgiving were shot
while walking and talking a mixture of English and Arabic in a
residential neighborhood. The shooter lived in a house on the street.*

Sparrows that fluttered and dipped by day
hunker under eaves, in crevices.
Juncos in charcoal capes have gone
to roost in shadowy evergreens.
Starlings are done with murmuration.

Darkness comes down off a porch,
deliberate as a bullet. Conversation
collapses. Words moan. The sidewalk
and the grass go red. Who can believe
in the birds now? Who can afford not to?

F-35 Flyover

The very air is roar,
a massive, unseen beast
enraged, a body blow;
sound waves shatter
the mind-wall. Rehearsal
for someone's somewhere
someday terror, somebody's
blood rain, a street, a village,
a city block obliterated
first by turbine thunder,
then exploding metal.

Never just one, but one-two-
three in measured order
ripping the blue, an unholy
trinity making sure all know
below the skin of thought
the all-powerful rule of spilled
blood. Even cemeteries shake
with it, cracks in the stones
of the already dead.

Who flies, who buys, who voted
for take-off, who practices
killing, who is far enough away,
or deaf to all caring?

Miranda's Rights

As you from crimes would pardon'd be,
Let your indulgence set me free.
                                    —*The Tempest*

The arresting self:

You have the right to remain silent
        about all you know that is unjust,
        but if you do, everything you don't say
        can and will be used against you.
        You may be safe from roaring winds,
        but days will numb you bland with ease,
        and nights will sweat you with dire dreams.

You have the right to an attorney.
        If you can't afford one, or even if you can,
        all the magic you were born or lucked into,
        like whiteness or good schools, won't
        spring you from soul's solitary, the island
        you come to despise, layer upon layer
        of comfort peeling in the salted air.

The arrested self:

You this, you that, I'm sick of your smug indictments.
        Do you blame just to mask your failure? Your fear
        of the grim sky? Birth and breeding made me
        an accomplice. I know that. But now I get to choose.
        Storm or no, I call for the mirror's mercy, time served
        for self-loathing. I call for will and means to mold
        with others new ways on the battered shore.

The Care of a Stranger

An unknown caller from Bangalore
or Nebraska, who knows, asks if I am David.
I am, says I, who are you? No name. Instead,
"I'm calling to confirm that you're having
pain and swelling in your feet, right?"

Well, no, but since you bring up hurts,
I have a pain in my head, and in my heart.
Oh, my heart aches. It aches for the poor,
the sick, the lonely, and of course it aches
for myself. Most of all for myself, I suppose.

Which is manageable. My aches, I mean.
I might not ache for all if my own were
not so manageable. Comfortable, almost,
my aches. I'm used to them, at least.
I can ache for you, too, if you like.

But pain in the feet? No, they're fine.
They move me along from one ache
to the next. Good day to you. I hope
you find someone who aches the way
you need. I hope it makes you feel better.

January 6, Feast of the Epiphany

The MAGi stormed the stable with their unbelief.
They said they'd followed a star. The animals
and shepherds hid in the stalls. Jesus wailed
and wailed. He was a newborn, after all.

His Father was a no-show, as usual.
Mom was scared but stood her ground.
She held the child, glared at the wise guys.
Joe the carpenter said little. It wasn't his time

yet. The wise guys crashed about. Made
quite a racket. The stable walls shook.
The wise guys yelled a lot, smashed the manger,
waved flags and smelly stuff they'd brought.

They said it was a gift, ha ha. Things got nasty.
Lots of the animals and shepherds were hurt.
Jesus kept crying, only now he had company.
All the animals. After a long while the wise guys

were pushed back, forced out of the stable.
The animals and shepherds returned to grazing,
sleeping, gathering, but something seemed off,
not right. It came to them, an epiphany, things

could never be as they were. Some essence
altered. The only hope — make a holy day
not to forget, make a promise, repair the stable,
care for the child, watch out for wise guys, pray.

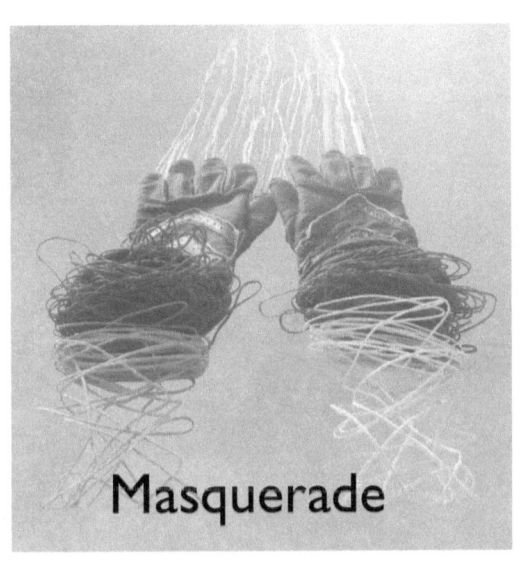

Masquerade

Pandemic Persona

We're all masked actors now.
Like lost members of a chorus
in an ancient Greek comedy
that fate has turned tragic,
we wander streets solo,
on the lookout for others,
wary when we find them
(hello, keep your distance),
seeking a script with an ending
other than our own.
Our syllables are muffled.
So much has to be repeated.
We've all become oracles.
We all speak in riddles,
puzzled by our own gibberish
in the dangerous air of day.

Every Day Is Halloween

Everyone dressed up as surgeons,
infectious disease doctors, nurses.
Everyone spooky as a ghost or ghoul.
Everyone warding off demons as of old.
Everyone dressed up as everyone.

Pandemic Pleasantries

"How are you?" lands like stone.
"Fine" is no breezy rejoinder.
"Take care" is a long flashing yellow.
"See you soon" has gone into hiding.
"So long" is a sober accounting.
At least now we mean what we say.

Guide for Wearing Masks in a Pandemic

In public wear one; bare-faced is no longer
     just a kind of lie, but a relief, a privilege, a statement.
     In general, show your mug as long as
     no one can see it.

It's okay to have mixed feelings about your mask.
     Sarcasm may be useful; irony, too, itself a covering.
     Ranting won't help. If you find yourself thinking of bandits,
     the Lone Ranger, or purdah, you need to keep thinking.

Be sure your mask covers both nose and mouth.
     Orifices in general are necessary but dangerous.
     If you have to sneeze, be a capped volcano:
     shudder and explode within.

Wash cloth masks before re-use. Microbes are seasoned
     survivors, with one job: replicate.
     Think of them as original sin on fertility pills.
     Baptize and baptize and baptize.

Expect to become confused at a reception when you're
     almost the only masked person there. When someone
     offers you wine and a cheese tray, try not to think
     about absurdity, dying, or the ethics of convenience.

Remember to stuff a mask in your pants pocket, jacket,
     satchel before you leave the house. Later, in a crowd
     when somehow you can't find one, roll your eyes,
     reflect on the workings of mystery and folly in human affairs.

Try not to get annoyed at your mask. It was a silly bit of material
until you came along. Like the virus itself,
a mask needs you to make sense of itself.
It needs you to hang on.

Laughter in the Time of Covid

I'm laughing so hard I start coughing.
What did the frog say to the saucepan?
You're not so hot.

I always wanted to be funny. Funny how
things turn out. The kid standing tall
on an electric skateboard looks funny,
like Jesus on water or Leonard DiCaprio
at the prow of the Titanic. The boy's on a roll
with a black mask over nose and mouth.
He looks like Zorro with a clothing failure.
If you're on the far right side of things
you tend to jam together at gatherings.
If on the left, you keep your distance.
How do you take an election poll?
You ask where people stand.

If heat kills Covid, the west should be
all better. This year it's pretty much
on fire. Wild! The blue states turned
flame red. Meanwhile, some reds
are turning blue, or at least purple.
Must be hard to breathe there.
Politics are funny, but get too close,
your sense of humor shrivels, like when
taste buds go dead, or smell shuts down.
Just about everybody is some kind of blue
these days, even if they don't notice.

What did the worker say to the billionaire?
It only hurts when I try to eat.
What did the eight billion say to the planet?
You're not so hot.
What did the planet say to the eight billion?
How's the breathing going?
It said,
There may not be much left to laugh about.
It said,
You ain't seen nothin' yet.
And the planet said,
Nothin' is no laughing matter.

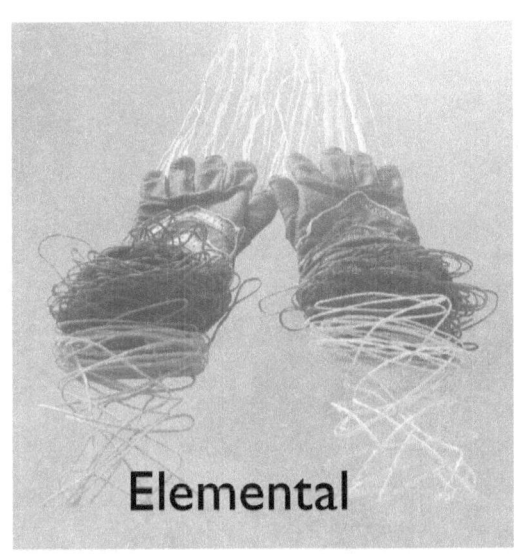

Elemental

Standard Time

Turn time
back an hour in fall, forestall
the morning dark.
Turn it
back, I mean ahead, in spring,
gather evening light. As if

time's our plaything, toss it
forth and back, and not
the other way around — us time's joke,
my wrinkles a punchline,
bark of an aging tree.

What's time anyway, an idea
or a body's
path through space? Tick. A step.
Tock. A step back. Tick.
Twirl the spindly
arms of the clock back fast enough,
you might meet

your long-gone parents. There's mom
at the kitchen sink, dad
getting off the bus from work,
your brothers squabbling
in the next room. And you,
at six setting
the table. Aren't I big now, to do it?
Turn back some more,

you're a floater in the womb, blind
       and wet and warm.

It's all right there, or here, whenever
   you want or let it, or when
it all comes knocking, not to be denied.
          It gathers in you,
     even what comes next
that you don't know. So the joke's
     on time after all. You're
never without dark, or light. Throw
   your watch away.
You've all the time there is.

Thumbs Up

...on the day so far. An early bike ride
along an unfamiliar country road.
When the Roman coliseum crowd
gave thumbs up as a gladiator
stood over his panting, beaten foe,
was it thumbs up let the poor slob live
or sword up – end him now?
Scholars and the movies disagree.
Who lives, who dies, by a finger's thrust?

Morning unfurls. July in Vermont,
whose name still mostly means
what it says. Elsewhere forests are burning.
Are they flammable or inflammable?
Elsewhere, not far away, people starve,
suffer violence or neglect. What disturbs
is how accustomed I've become to blazing
contradictions. I'm not even that disturbed,
which disturbs me still more.

The high-low cooing of a dove, a sad sweet
song that uplifts somehow like the blues.
For years I thought: morning, not mourning.
How to praise the essential blaze,
the daily sanction of the sun? I pedal by
two weathered signs on a single pole,
"Entrance Road" and "No Outlet".
I laugh and give thumbs up.

Heatwave

The air thick and hot as my own blood.
    Invisible steamy ocean outside,
a sluggish river within. Both sides
    of the beleaguered flesh straining
the hungry lungs and clamoring cells.

If only I can remember, after the wave
    breaks, so little separates
these climates out and in,
    just a thin fevered membrane
crying from all pores.

I can't breathe

says the black man dying on the street.

I can't breathe,
says the Covid patient, gasping, beat.

I can't breathe,
says the body politic, choking on tweets.

I can't breathe,
says the planet. The stifling heat!

Breathwork

Think of the Carboniferous as a sixty-million year inhale by plants, sucking carbon dioxide from the sky, and the last two hundred years as a monstrous human-engineered exhale, undoing what the plants did so long ago.

—Rebecca Solnit, *Orwell's Roses*

More like hyperventilate than exhale. Eight billion of us on a breathless rush to the cliff's edge.
If roots and leaves could talk — they do, if we have ears to hear – calm down,
they say, what's the rush, take your time, they say. Time gives and takes
us all, they say. The trick, they say, slow down, keep the ground in view.
Balance, they say, breathe in, breathe out, what's taken in, replace, what's used, repair,
study the cadence of sea and clouds, the murmuration of starlings, fair relations between us,
hold to what is green, they say, the mystery of our undergrowth, the leafy laughter of trees.

Please

You're so calm.
 I hear that a lot.
The burning world!
 What can I say?
How can you say *that?*
 Do you see flames?
Yes! Everywhere!
 After flames, smoldering.
How can you think about after?
 There's energy
 in smolder.
What about *right now?*
 My heart
 once nearly
 stopped,
 it was so
 blocked.
What does that have to do...
 Just in time I got
 a work-around,
 a bypass.
 Even then
 they said
 I was so calm.
The roof just caved in!
 Oh, I know.
 But not "just".
 Long ago.
So strange! You seem...
 Yes. Funny,

I don't feel it.
We need to do something!
    Please look harder.
Where?
    My eyes.
I'm looking. I don't get it.
    What do you see?
Flames! Everywhere!

No words

i

to touch the beauty of
fall's tired, tall grasses
waving, or the maple leaves
fallen, silently on fire.

Still we try, as if to mirror
the grace of decline might
halt it, or in sharing the mind's
stained glass, overcome.

Like sweaty kids chasing
one more ball who pretend
not to hear the call to come in
as darkness falls.

ii

Quilt, mosaic, rug, yeah, yeah,
perfect yellow-red beneath
their tree, magicians of renewal,
etc. They'd hoot at all I utter,

if they could or cared.
Forget it, they might say,
except they never, just relaxing
as themselves. Heavy lifting

done, ease of decay. Color,
shape, like music, no reason.
If I just be quiet, can I
lie down with you, leaves?

Morning after the Storm

Snow thunders off the roof,
              a freight train off its rails;
frozen boxcars mash the juniper as they thud.

So much on the brink,
              so much losing grip, just a smidge
of shift or melt and the whole shebang unhinged.

I've a doomsday head. And now
              the sun. Icicles point and glint,
drip their own demise, unbothered. Behind them,

beneath the eaves, stalactite shadows mural
              the light-struck siding.
Always an underside, a story behind the story.

Earthshine

*...the faint illumination of the dark, larger portion of a
crescent moon when earth reflects light from the sun onto it.*

You see a glow,
however muted,
coming from
my dark side?
Of course, it really
comes from you,
gathered from
your own turning.

This night
we move in each
other's orbit.
Whose light
is whose?
Who casts,
who counters
shadow?

We linger,
grateful, do not
know or need
to know
who gives,
who receives,
who is one,
two, one.

Stardust

Who says stars aren't born?
A nebula of gas and dust,
pregnant for a million years,
hotter and hotter in cosmic
labor till nuclear reactions
burst with light. An astral
infant of hydrogen and helium
shines in universal night.

So why should I be surprised
to wake up again, dawn
slanting across the bed
a bit earlier than yesterday?
March is bent on equalizing
day and night. But I'm off-
kilter, working myself into
a protracted dust-storm
of lost days. The season
taunts me with its balance.
If only I could learn, maybe
my dark's a counter-weight,
a low-pitched necessary whine
against the hum of my routines,
the totter to my teeter.

The murk where new star grew
falls away like placenta.
It might morph into a planet,
like earth, sun's afterbirth,
where I fuss in my slow burn,
draw back the curtain, squint
at near blinding equilibrium.

A Roll in Oakledge Park

By a lake whose waters were once a sea
formed after the melt of mile-thick ice,
in a park of graceful oaks a mother teaches
her young son how to roll down a gentle hill.
Lying flat in the grass, arms stretched above
his head like a diver, he lets gravity take over.

Beneath the giggling child, beneath the grass,
beneath the underworld tangle of roots, sand,
and soil, long silent shelves of Monkton Quartzite,
500 million years old, showing reddish gray
and purple where slabs have heaved up
along the ragged shore. Beneath and far more
beneath, mostly molten magma, 1800 miles thick,
and below that, mostly superheated liquid
iron and nickel, 1400 miles deep, and still farther
below that, at the inner core, a hot dense ball
of mostly iron 750 more miles to the center.

There, depth in one sense stops. Except
it's all a tiny sphere turning over and over
1000 mph and spinning 67,000 mph through
darkness with no known outer reach – this bit
of rock with so many forms and unlikely fragile
atmosphere breathed in and out by the small
tumbling boy and his mother laughing merrily
in the grass of their singular moment.

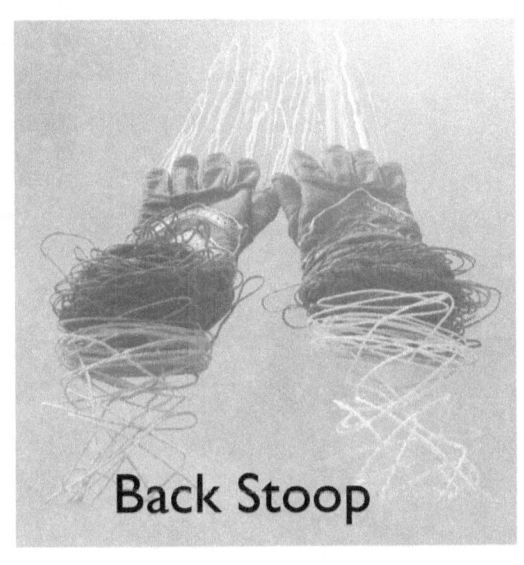

Back Stoop

Inklings

The rear stoop, time-honored as a place for reflection or chatting with neighbors, and here we are. Hard to believe. I mean that broadly. It's hard sometimes to keep faith. Life kicks our butts pretty often, and sometimes viciously, out of the blue. Another day, if we're lucky, it gives us a high five, wraps us in feelings of connection, satisfaction, gratitude. Confusing. A mysterious mix of struggle and ease, daily grind and wonder.

Poems, whether I'm writing or reading them, are one of the ways I try to keep faith. Maybe they work that way for you, too. I don't look to them to contain or express certainties, though they may at times. I'm chasing life, pure and gloriously un-simple. To engage with life and have each poem embody a bit of it — not describe, or translate, or imitate it, but be an active force, an experience. And an offering.

I'll never fully get there. I know that. But whether in poems or the extraordinary odyssey of daily living, maybe there are inklings and instants, bright and fleeting, the kind where ice and heat collide, the instant of thaw. Awe.

In hope of that blessing, I plan not to let go. I hope you don't, either. Let me end by saying, with only a small wink, Please Hold.

Acknowledgments

I'm grateful to many for help in making this book. Thanks, first of all, to Sharon Webster, my partner in art and life, for her love and support, for the example of a vibrant, creative life, and for pulling me back from revising certain poems into oblivion. Thanks, too, for the use of a detail from her stunning art piece, "Handed Down," on the cover.

Thank you to a number of dear friends who offered invaluable comments on individual poems and the book as a whole: Greg Delanty, Antonello Borra, Peter Burns, and Richard Harrison.

Deep thanks to Donna Bister and Marc Estrin, visionary publishers of Fomite Press. It was a shock and great sadness when Marc died not long after this book went into production. I am full of gratitude for his friendship and for giving us all the example of his remarkable life and questing spirit. They continue to inspire. Thank you, Marc, and thank you, Donna, for supporting my work and that of so many other writers, and for reminding us that art lives beyond the confines of the conventional publishing world.

Finally, thanks to the editors of publications or venues where some of these poems have appeared: *Avenue*; *Ethic=Visceral*; *Seven Days*; Poem City Montpelier display and anthologies 2024 and 2023; Poem Town Randolph display and anthology 2024; Poetry Walk 2023, organized by the Burnham Memorial Library and the Vermont State Parks; and *Vital Signs*, from Fomite Press.

About the Author

Dave Cavanagh is an American/
Canadian transplanted to Vermont
from Montreal by way of Ontario.
He feels blessed to have landed in
fertile soil. His ancestors immigrated
to Canada from Ireland in the late
1820s. His parents worked their way
out of poverty in post-World War
II Montreal. In elementary and high
school, most of Dave's classmates were
recent immigrants from various parts of Europe, especially Italy. Only
later did he realize how formative and broadening that experience was
for him. He feels privileged to find his nationality defined less by bor-
ders than by his relationships —with family, friends, language, history,
and the physical world. He has no answer for those who consider his
passion for cycling to be obsessive. He just pedals away.

Please Hold is Dave's sixth book of poems. His poetry has been
nominated for a Pushcart Prize and has also appeared in numerous
journals and anthologies in the U.S., Canada, and Europe. He has
taught literature, writing, and interdisciplinary studies at colleges
in Vermont and Ontario. For many years Dave was an associate
dean and co-director of an award-winning bachelor's program for
non-traditional learners at Johnson State College (now Vermont
State University - Johnson). He lives in Burlington with his part-
ner, the visual artist and poet Sharon Webster.

Fomite

Fomite

Writing a review on social media sites for readers will help the progress of independent publishing. To submit a review, go to the book page on any of the sites and follow the links for reviews. Books from independent presses rely on reader-to-reader communications.

For more information or to order any of our books, visit:

http://www.fomitepress.com/our-books.html

More poetry from Fomite...

Warren Baker
  Shadow Light
Anna Blackmer
  Hexagrams
L. Brown
  Loopholes
Sue D. Burton
  Little Steel
Christine Butterworth-McDermott
  Evelyn As
  The Spellbook of Fruit and Flowers
David Cavanagh
  Cycling in Plato's Cave
  Please Hold
Rajnesh Chakrapani
  The Repetition of Exceptional Weeks
James Connolly
  Picking Up the Bodies
Benjamin Dangl
  A World Where Many Worlds Fit
Greg Delanty
  Behold the Garden
  Loosestrife
Mason Drukman
  Drawing on Life
J. C. Ellefson
  Foreign Tales of Exemplum and Woe

Fomite

Fomite

Fomite

Scott T. Starbuck
  Carbonfish Blues
  Hawk on Wire
  Industrial Oz
Seth Steinzor
  Among the Lost
  Once Was Lost
  To Join the Lost
  The Dragon of Sassafras Mountain
Susan Thomas
  In the Sadness Museum
  Silent Acts of Public Indiscretion
  The Empty Notebook Interrogates Itself
Sharon Webster
  Everyone Lives Here
  O Song
Tony Whedon
  The Tres Riches Heures
  The Falkland Quartet
Claire Zoghb
  Dispatches from Everest

More dual language titles from Fomite
Vito Bonito/Alison Grimaldi Donahue
  Soffiata Via/Blown Away
Antonello Borra
  Erbario/lapidario
Antonello Borra/Blossom Kirschenbaum
  Alfabestiario
  AlphaBetaBestiaro
Antonello Borra/Anis Memon
  Fabbrica delle idee/The Factory of Ideas
Alessio Brandolini/Giorgio Mobili
  Miniature Cities
Lorenzo Carlucci/Todd Portnowitz
  Methods

Fomite

Jeannette Clariond/Lawrence Schimel
  Desert Memory
Silvia Comoglio/Giorgio Mobili
  Via Crucis
Tina Escaja/Mark Eisner
  Caída Libre/Free Fall
Luigi Fontanella/Giorgio Mobili
  L'Adolescenza e la notte/Adolescence and Night
JohannesHösle/Marc Estrin
  Album aus Dietenbronn/Whatever Befalls
Aristea Papalexandrou/Philip Ramp
  Μας προσπερνά/It's Overtaking Us
Katerina Anghelaki-Rooke/Philip Ramp
  Losing Appetite for Existence
Mikis Theodoraksi/Gail Holst-Warhaft
  The House with the Scorpions
Paolo Valesio/Todd Portnowitz
  La Mezzanotte di Spoleto/Midnight in Spoleto

www.ingramcontent.com/pod-product-compliance
Lightning Source LLC
Chambersburg PA
CBHW030500130626
46549CB00007B/2800